Weak Forms

A pronunciation practice book

Colin Mortimer

Drawings by Daria Gan

Cambridge University Press

Cambridge

London   New York   New Rochelle

Melbourne   Sydney

Published by the Press Syndicate of the University of Cambridge
The Pitt Building, Trumpington Street, Cambridge CB2 1RP
32 East 57th Street, New York, NY 10022, USA
296 Beaconsfield Parade, Middle Park, Melbourne 3206, Australia

First published 1977
Reprinted 1979, 1980

Set, printed and bound in Great Britain by
Fakenham Press Limited, Fakenham, Norfolk

ISBN 0 521 21627 3   Book
ISBN 0 521 21760 1   Cassette

Contents

3

Selected combinations of two weak forms

Selected combinations of three weak forms

Introduction

A good practical grasp of the weak forms of English is essential to good pronunciation and listening comprehension. This practice book contains fifty dialogues in which some of the more important weak forms are contextualised. The items selected are all weak forms containing the 'neutral' vowel. The first twenty-eight dialogues feature individual weak forms. The remaining dialogues are devoted to a selection of sequences of two or three of the items that have first been treated individually. The pronunciation of each weak form is indicated in phonetic transcription, in the heading. *Featured items are identified in the text in a lighter type face. An asterisk after a word indicates that it should be pronounced in its strong form.* It is not possible in such a short book to give explanations of the circumstances in which weak and strong forms are appropriate:

eg. *the* – /ðə/ only before consonant sounds.

from – strong in final position.

that – all demonstratives strong.

Phonetics handbooks will readily provide the relevant basic information, and should be consulted. A short selection of suitable books is listed at the end of this Introduction.

Using the book

Students should be given plenty of opportunity to understand the dialogues and to hear them spoken both in their entirety and in sections by a good model or models. Although the items on which particular dialogues focus are indicated in phonetic transcription, a reliable model, either in person or on tape, is essential.

When students have heard the whole dialogue, they can practise individual phrases containing the featured weak forms. Note that it is dangerous to practise a weak item *in isolation*, because it is difficult to avoid pronouncing isolated words strongly. When individual phrases have been practised, longer sections can be done until a satisfactory performance of a whole dialogue is attained. Dialogues should be regularly revised, and some may usefully be memorised.

5

The weak forms on which a dialogue is concentrating appear in lighter type. There may, however, be words not in light type which need to be pronounced weakly if the dialogue is to be spoken properly. Most of such items are featured specifically elsewhere in the book, and their incidental occurrence in other dialogues can be treated as useful revision or as a foretaste. But primary attention should be given to the weak forms actually specified in the heading.

The recording

The dialogues are recorded on cassette, and each dialogue is preceded by a short *listen and repeat* section, with gaps on the tape for student repetition. In this preliminary section, the weak forms to be used in the dialogue are drilled. The dialogues themselves are, of course, recorded without gaps, but teachers with a class, or students working individually, can use the pause and rewind mechanisms of their machines to play and repeat sections on which they wish to concentrate.

Paced reading: Students often find it helpful to read *along with* the tape. To do this kind of paced reading, it may be advisable to turn down the volume of the tape a little.

Other work

Answering suitable questions about the dialogues, or summarising them, is a useful way of consolidating pronunciation gains consciously made, since it diverts a measure of attention to meaning.

A number of the dialogues are *implicatory* in style, in that something in them is left unsaid, and students may enjoy finding words to express their inferences:

eg. *Dialogue 23* Implication: Dad, also, has made a bad purchase.
Dialogue 24 Implication: The gift wasn't worth stealing.

Select basic reading

Gimson, A. C., *An Introduction to the Pronunciation of English*, Edward Arnold
Jones, D., *An Outline of English Phonetics*, Cambridge
MacCarthy, P. A. D., *The Teaching of Pronunciation*, Cambridge
O'Connor, J. D., *Better English Pronunciation*, Cambridge

Pring, J. T., *Colloquial English Pronunciation*, Longman
Windsor Lewis, J., *A Guide to English Pronunciation*,
    Universitetsforlaget, Oslo

Key to phonetic symbols

Vowels and diphthongs

i	*as in*	see /si/	ɜ	*as in*	fur /fɜ(r)/
ɪ	*as in*	sit /sɪt/	ə	*as in*	ago /ə/ˈɡəʊ/
e	*as in*	ten /ten/	eɪ	*as in*	page /peɪdʒ/
æ	*as in*	hat /hæt/	əʊ	*as in*	home /həʊm/
ɑ	*as in*	arm /ɑm/	aɪ	*as in*	five /faɪv/
o	*as in*	got /got/	aʊ	*as in*	now /naʊ/
ɔ	*as in*	saw /sɔ/	ɔɪ	*as in*	join /dʒɔɪn/
ʊ	*as in*	put /pʊt/	ɪə	*as in*	near /nɪə(r)/
u	*as in*	too /tu/	eə	*as in*	hair /heə(r)/
ʌ	*as in*	cup /kʌp/	ʊə	*as in*	pure /pjʊə(r)/

Consonants

p	*as in*	pen /pen/	s	*as in*	so /səʊ/
b	*as in*	bad /bæd/	z	*as in*	zoo /zu/
t	*as in*	tea /ti/	ʃ	*as in*	she /ʃi/
d	*as in*	did /dɪd/	ʒ	*as in*	vision /vɪʒn/
k	*as in*	cat /kæt/	h	*as in*	how /haʊ/
ɡ	*as in*	get /ɡet/	m	*as in*	man /mæn/
tʃ	*as in*	chin /tʃɪn/	n	*as in*	no /nəʊ/
dʒ	*as in*	June /dʒun/	ŋ	*as in*	sing /sɪŋ/
f	*as in*	fall /fɔl/	l	*as in*	leg /leɡ/
v	*as in*	voice /vɔɪs/	r	*as in*	red /red/
θ	*as in*	thin /θin/	j	*as in*	yes /jes/
ð	*as in*	then /ðen/	w	*as in*	wet /wet/

I should like to express my thanks to Peter MacCarthy and Leonard Tibbitts for helpful comment and encouragement while I was writing this book, and I am especially grateful to Jack Windsor Lewis for robust clarification and reinforcement of my already strongly held views about the importance of weak forms. Also I wish to thank Sidney Whitaker for constructive suggestions when I was considering typographic aspects.

1   a /ə/

A   **So what went wrong?**

B   **Well, you said all I needed was** a **pencil,** a **ruler,** a **piece of wood,** a **saw,** a **hammer and** a **couple of nails.**

A   **I said you needed** a **pencil,** a **ruler,** a **piece of wood,** a **saw,** a **hammer,** a **couple of nails, and** a **bit of common** *sense*.†

B   **Ah.**

     † Words in italics should be given extra emphasis.

2   an /ən/

A   **I need** an **immediate answer.**

B   **You shall have** an **answer. In** an **hour or so.**

A   **I must have** an **answer now.**

B   **It's not** an **easy decision to make. But if you insist on** an **immediate answer, it must be** an **extremely reluctant 'no'.**

A   **Oh.**

B   **Sorry.**

A   **Well, I suppose if you** *do* **need** an **extra hour or so . . .**

B   **But I don't, now, do I?** An **extra drink, yes. Have one? Before you go?**

3   the /ðə/†

A   **Now the* exercise – the drill.**
    LISTEN: The **pear**, the **peach**, the **pineapple**.
    The* apple, the* orange, the* apricot.
    REPEAT.
B   The **pear**, the **peach**, the **pineapple**.
    The* apple, the* orange, the* apricot.
A   The **father**, the **mother**. The* **uncle**, the* **aunt**.
B   The **father**, the **mother**. The* **uncle**, the* **aunt**.
A   REVISION: **Apple. Pear.**
B   **The* apple. The pear.**
A   **Good.** NEW WORD: **End.**
B   **The* end.**
A   **Good.**
B   **Good.**

   † Only before consonant sounds.

I I

4 some /səm/

A Mm! Delicious, John! Can I have some **more**?
How d'you make it, by the way?

B Oh, you need some **lean meat**, some **vegetables**, some **butter**,
flour, salt. Chillies. Some **garlic**, if you've got some*. Lots of
things.

A **Who gave you the recipe?**

B Oh, some* woman I know.

A **Well, it really** *is* some* dish!

B **So is** *she*! **Now, you did say you wanted** some **more, darling?**

A **Well . . . if I'm to have** some **pudding, perhaps not.**

5 and /ən(d)/

A A **whisky** and **soda.** A **whisky** and **water.** A **brandy** and **soda.**
Three gin and **tonics with ice** and **lemon,** and **two gin** and
tonics *without* **ice** and **lemon.** And **another whisky** and **soda.**
And **a glass of water for me.**

B A **whisky** and **soda.** A **whisky** and **water.** A **brandy** and **soda.**
Three gin and **tonics with ice** and **lemon,** and **two gin** and
tonics *without* **ice** and **lemon.** And **another whisky** and **soda.**
And **a glass of water for you, sir. Right, sir.**

A **No, wait a minute. Let me change that. Let's have . . .**

6 but /bət/

A But **I** can't. **I'm** sorry, but **I** can't.
B But **you must.**
A **I'd like** to. But **I** can't.
B But **I'm** depending on you. We're *all* depending on you.
A **I'll** do *anything* but that.
B But *no* one else could do it as well as **you**!
A Why not ask **Dalia**? She could do it even *better*.
B But she's too *busy*.

7 of /əv/

A There you are, Betty – a bottle of milk. Three boxes of matches.
A can of beans. Two bags of sugar. A packet of biscuits. A jar of
jam. A bottle of lemon squash. And two tins of peaches.
That's the lot, I think. OK?
B Thanks, dear. How much was it? Ugh! What's this in the bottom
of the bag?
A Oh, yes. And half a dozen eggs.

8 to /tə/

A **I have** to go out.
B **Where** to*?
A To **see** somebody.
B To **see** Nigel, I suppose.
A **You'll have** to learn to mind your own business.
B *You'll* have to learn that you *are* my business.
A **I'm** not your property, though.
B **I** told Nigel to keep away from you. And if he doesn't, **I'm** going
to punch his . . .
A **I'm** going to see your little friend, Susan, if you want to know.
B Susan? Why?
A To scratch her eyes out.
B To do *what*?
A **I'll** attend to *you* when I get back.

13

9 for /fə(r)/†

A   Do it for *my* sake.

B   Not for **you**, not for **Mum**, not for **Dad**, not for **anybody** – not even for **myself**, thank you very much!

A   *I* know who you'll do it for*! For **dear little Elizabeth**!

B   Oh, for **heaven's sake**, shut up!

A   Haven't seen her recently. Had a quarrel?

B   For *that*, I'm going to . . .

A   I didn't mean it, Dick, honestly! Stop it! Oh! Ouch!

B   That's for **being** *cheeky*!

A   Anyway, she's got awful teeth! Ouch! And she's bowlegged!

† Linking 'r' before vowel sounds – see *Link-up*.

10 from /frəm/

A   I had a call from **Bill**.

B   From **Bill**? Who's **Bill**?

A   He's very special. He telephones me from **overseas**. Every day.

B   Where from*?

A   Oh – from **wherever** he happens to be: Africa, America, Asia . . . From **Australia**, this time.

B   He *must* be special.

A   He hates to be away from **me**.

B   Of course, George sometimes rings *me* from the factory. The trouble is, *he* always reverses the *charges*!

A   Oh, *Bill* reverses the charges, of course.

11 at /ət/

A   **Where were you at one o'clock?**

B   At **one o'clock?** At **my mother's.**

A   At **two o'clock?**

B   At **my sister's.**

A   **And** at **one thirty?**

B   At **one thirty, Officer?** At **a point approximately half way**
     between my mother's and my sister's.

A   At **Sam's Bar, in fact?**

B   **Only for five minutes,** at **the most. Why?**

12 them /ðəm/

A I saw them **together**.
B *Where* **did you see** them?
A **In the town.**
B *When* **did you see** them?
A **This morning.**
B **Did you** *say* **anything to** them?
A **I told** them **I should tell you.**
B **Which you've now done. Thank you.**
A **Aren't you going to send for** them?
B **No need. I've already invited** them **for dinner.**
A *Them**? **Both of** them? **Together?**
B **Like to join us?**

13 us /əs/

A **Let's ask him to let** us **go.**
B **He won't let** us **go.**
A **He can't keep** us **forever.**
B **Course he can.**
A **Let's escape.**
B **He'd catch** us. **Anyway, I like it here. He treats** us **well. Gives**
   us **lovely clothes. Lovely food – everything.**
A **He must give** us **our** *freedom*!
B **Don't be greedy.**

14 that /ðət/

A **We all know** that **we face problems. We know** that **we face**
   difficulties. We are all aware that **the difficulties** that **we face are**
   not difficulties that **will be overcome immediately, or** that **will be**
   overcome easily. We all recognise that **the problems** that
   confront us are not problems that **will be solved overnight. But**
   I sometimes wonder if we realise . . . if we realise *sufficiently*
   that . . .
B **That** *that** **was the clock striking** *two*, **Frank! Go to sleep!**
A **Sorry, dear. Didn't know it was so late. My big day, tomorrow,**
   you know. Ah, well. Goodnight.
B **It's a lovely speech, Frank.**

15 as /əz/

A **As John couldn't come, he asked me to come** as **a substitute.**
But *you're* not *Julie.*

B **No.** As **Julie couldn't come, she sent me** – as **a substitute.**

A **You know, it looks to me** as **if John and Julie . . .**

B **It does, doesn't it?**

A **I disapprove of such tricks,** as **a rule.**

B **So do I.** As **a rule.**

A **However, . . .**

B **Well?**

16 as . . . as /əz . . . əz/

A **You're** as **cunning** as **a fox.**

B **Cunning? I'm** as **innocent** as **a child!**

A **And** as **slippery** as **a snake!**

B **Anyway, believe me, this necklace is unique! And old! Old** as
the hills!

A **And gold?**

B As *good* **as.***

* Probably strong in this final position, but in very familiar speech
could be weak.

17 than /ðən/

A   Carol's more sensible than Jenny, prettier than Jenny, cleverer than Jenny, and richer than Jenny. So why do I like Jenny more than Carol?

B   And why does Jenny like *me* more than you?

18 there /ðə(r)/

A   There ought to be someone here.

B   There ought to be. But there isn't, I don't think.

A   There's /ðəz/ a light in that room.

B   Let's take a look.

A   Oh, my God!

B   Mm. It looks as if there's someone here after all, poor chap. There's a phone over there. Better ring the police.

19 am /əm/†

A   Why am I leaving? Where am I going? Who am I going with? Where am I staying? When am I coming back? *Am** I coming back? These are questions you'll probably wish to ask me, Barbara, but . . .

B   Now, darling. How am I looking?

     † For 'I'm' – see *Contractions*.

20 are /ə(r)/†

A   These are the best.

B   These are nice, too.

A   Mm. But these are more suitable, don't you think?

B   They're a bit old-fashioned, perhaps.

A   And they're a bit flashy, I suppose.

B   They are*, yes. Anyway, there are no more in the shop. And we *must* give them their present today.

A   So what are we going to do?

B   Well, Freddie and Paulette are *both* a bit old-fashioned, you know.

A   Yes. But in a flashy sort of way.

     † 'They're', 'we're' etc. – see *Contractions*.

21 was /wəz/

A The man was *kind*.
B He was **generous**.
A He *was**. Extremely **generous**.
B He was **popular**.
A Oh, he was very very **popular**.
B So when we heard he was . . .
A **Yes.**
B I was . . .
A We *all* **were.**

22 has /əz/†

A The bus has **gone already, Janet.**
B **Which** has **gone? The Sixty?**
A **The Sixty Six** has **gone as well.**
B **It must have gone early, unless my watch** has **stopped. Look –**
   Madge has **missed it too. And Rose** has **missed it. No use**
   running, Rose!
A **Gosh –** *Rose* has **put on a pound or two since she last ran for a**
   bus! Oops! No use running, Rose! It's gone!

   † 'He's', 'Jack's', etc. – see *Contractions.*

23   have /əv/†

A   **The wheels** have **dropped off! The wings** have **broken! It's useless!**
B   **How many times** have **you flown it?**
A   **Only once! I wouldn't** have **bought it if I'd known!**
B   **And I suppose if** *they* **hadn't known, they wouldn't** have **reduced it to half price. Anyway, we all** have* **to learn, eh? Oh, by the way, I've bought you this. Got it from Walker's. Like it?**
A   **Oh, it's marvellous, Dad. Thanks. They had one in Gray's sale, but I couldn't afford it. Thanks, Dad.**

† 'I've', 'you've'. etc. – see *Contractions*.

24   had /əd/†

A   **All our money** had **gone.**
B   **My jewels** had **gone.**
A   **Our clothes** had **gone.**
B   **The passports** had **gone.**
A   **The air tickets** had **gone.**
B   **Everything** had **been taken.**
A   **Everything we** had*. **It'd all gone.**
B   **Except the present we'd bought you.**
A   **They hadn't taken that, fortunately.**
B   **Hope you like it.**

† 'We'd', 'you'd', etc. – see *Contractions*.

25 does /dəz/

A He *does** sound nice. But I hope you won't mind if I ask him a few questions, Millicent, such as where does he . . .

B Where does he live? What sort of family does he come from? Who . . . *Whom* does he know that *we* know? What does he do for a living? How much money does he make? That sort of thing, you mean, mother?

A Yes, dear. And also what does . . .

B What does he see in *me*?

A Apart from your money, dear, yes.

26 shall /ʃəl(ʃl)/†

A Where shall I say I've been?

B The cinema.

A Who shall I say I've been with?

B Your sister. Where shall we meet tomorrow?

A Same place. Shall* we?

B Mm. When shall we meet? Same time?

A And what shall we do?

B Same thing?

A Lovely.

     † 'We'll', 'he'll', etc. – see *Contractions.*

27 can /kən/

A She can **play the flute.** She can **paint pictures.** She can **write poems.** She can **grow plants.** She can **do** *most* **things.** What can *I* do? I can't do *any* of the things *she* can*!

B You can **fight.**

A Yes, but who wants a girl who can **fight?**

B *I* do.

A   **Tell me what I** must **do.**

B   **You** must **go to them. And you** must **confess. Tell them it was**
*you***.**

A   **I suppose I** must*****.

B   **You** must *trust* **them. They'll be lenient, I'm sure.**

A   **Yes. Yes, I suppose I** must **tell them** *everything*.

B   **Well, perhaps not** *quite* **everything.**

A   **Oh?**

B   **No need to mention** *me*, **for instance.**

SELECTED COMBINATIONS
OF TWO WEAK FORMS†

29 /əv + ə, ən, ðə, səm, əs, ðəm/

A **You hate all** of them.
B **No. But I dislike** *one* **of them. Roger, I think his name is.**
A **Because** of the **way he dresses, I suppose.**
B **No. Because** of a *word* **he used in front** of an **old lady.**
A **Oh, yes. I heard. But she's so old-***fashioned***!**
B **Some** of us *are*, **I suppose. And anyway, it's hardly a** *new* **word, is it?**

30 /tə + ðə, ðəm/

A **All those friends of yours overseas – why not write** to them? **Or** *go* **somewhere. Go** to the **cinema. Or** to the **beach. Or** to the **tennis club. You** *can't* **sit brooding about that girl all the time.**
B **Yes, I think I** *will* **write** to them.
A **Good.**
B **She usually goes** to the **Post Office about five.**

† Where *single* weak forms from the selected *pairs* occur, these are also identified in the text.

31 /ət + ə, ən, ðə, ðəm/

A 'Stop *screeching*', did you say? Don't you know I once sang at a concert? At an inter*national* concert? At the biggest theatre in town? You must look at my press cuttings!

B I *will* look at them, darling. But I have to be at a meeting at a quarter past seven. And I *would* like a bath. Do hurry up. Please!

32 /fə(r) + ə, ðə, səm/

A How long have I come for*? For a month. Why have I come? Oh . . . for some sunshine. For the sea. For some good food. For the wine. For a bit of excitement, I suppose. Why did *you* come?

B For the money. I work here.

A Not *all* the time, I hope.

33 /frəm + ə, ən, ðə, səm, ðəm/

A   I got it from an **old friend, who got it** from a **friend, who got it** from some **friends, who borrowed it** from the **Browns. Where did you get the idea it was** *stolen* **from them?**

B   I got it from a **friend.** A **mutual friend.**

34 /ə(r) + ə, ən, ðə, səm/

A   These are a **new type. And those** are the **type you had before. Oh – here** are some **more. These** are the **very latest. And the best. Just arrived.**

B   Yes, I can see those are an **entirely different model. Where are** the **handles, by the way?**

A   Oh, er . . . Modern design, you see. No handles. No handles *needed*, you see.

B   Mm. Ah! What are the *plastic* things in the bottom of the box?

A   Plas . . . Oh, yes. Optional extras, you see.

35 /wəz + ə, ən, ðə, səm/

A   *That* was a **poor meal.**

B   It was an *extremely* **poor meal.**

A   The soup was a **disgrace.**

B   The meat was the **toughest ever.**

A   All we got for pudding was some **tinned fruit.**

B   Where was the **special sauce?**

A   Where was the **special dessert?**

B   Nothing was the **same as last year.**

A   Except the bill.

B   And *that* was a bit bigger, actually.

36 /wə(r) + ə, ən, ðə/

A   **You** were a **star**. **You** were the **greatest actress of your
generation**. **You** were the **most beautiful woman of your time**.
You were an **inspiration to us all**.

B   And *you* were an **incorrigible liar, Rupert**.

A   **Beatrice!**

B   **You still** *are*, **thank God**.

37   /ðə(r) + ə(r), wə(r)/

A   There were **five**.

B   There were **four**.

A   There were **five**. At *least* **five**.

B   There were **only four**.

A   **Well, anyway,** *one* **thing's certain**.

B   **What?**

A   There are **only four now**.

B   There are **only** *three*, **in fact**.

SELECTED COMBINATIONS OF THREE WEAK FORMS†

38 /ən(d), bət + əv + ə, ən, ðə, səm/

A **The Company Chairman reminded everybody** of the **problems we face.**

B And of the **difficulties before us.**

A And of the **hard road that lies ahead.**

B And of an **ever increasing need to make sacrifices.**

A And of a **need to increase our efforts.**

B **He spoke not only** of the **problems.**

A But of the **new opportunities.**

B And of the **new challenges.**

A And of some **recent plans.**

B And of a **bright future.**

A And of a **bright, though distant future.**

† Where *pairs* from the selected *threes* occur, these are also identified in the text.

39 /ən(d), bət + tə + ðə, səm/

A **I went** to the **Scotts** and to the **Greens** and to the **Smalls,** and
to the **rest of the places on your list. Oh** – but to the *Bonds*, I
couldn't go – they've gone on holiday.

B **You went** to the **Smiths** and to the **Grants, of course?**

A **Yes.** And to some *new* people next door to the **Grants. They
donated more than** *anyone*. **More than the Grants, even.**

B **The Grants won't like** *that*! **I must tell them. Tactfully.**

A **I told them. And gave them a second chance!**

B **What did you say?**

A **I said: 'The new people have given a lot more than you.'**

B **I see.**

40 /ən(d), bət + ət + ə, ðə/

A **George wasn't** at the **meeting,** but at a **party. A** *wild* **one.**

B **Not** at the **meeting?** And at a **wild party? How disgraceful!
Where?**

A **In town.** And at the **house of a friend of yours** – **Josephine. You
really must speak to George.**

B **I shall** *certainly* **do that. But at the moment,** *she's* **the one I must
speak to! At Josephine's you say? And at a wild party** *I* **wasn't
invited to?**

41 /ən(d), bət + fə(r) + ə, ðə, səm/

A   I **know** why you **came** – you **came** for a **drink,** and for some **food,** and for a **talk with the boys,** and for the **television.**

B   I *swear* I **came here not** for a **drink** and for the **various other things you mention,** but for the **chance to see your pretty, smiling face again!**

A   **Oh, Victor!**

B   **So bring the food and drink, and switch on the television, and tell me where the boys are, my darling** – there's a **good girl.**

42   /ən(d), bət + frəm + ə, ən, ðə/

A   From the **family I got** *this,* and from a **colleague I got** *that,* and from an **old friend I got** *these,* and from some **other friends I got** *these.* But from the *boss* I got *this*! **Look! Isn't it marvellous!**

B   **Mm.** And from the **look of it, you'd better be** *careful*!

43 /ər + ət + ə, ðə/

A My **parents** are at a **meeting and my sisters** are at the **cinema.
I'm all alone. Like to join me?**

B **Sorry, but** *my* **parents** are at the **theatre, and my little sisters** are
at the **moment expecting me to bath them and put them to bed.**

A **Oh.**

B **Like to read them a story?**

44 /wəz + ət + ə, ən, ðə/

A **Last year it** was at a **restaurant. The year before, it** was at an
expensive hotel, and the year before that, it was at the **factory
itself – in the canteen. And that was the** *best* **party, I thought.**

B **Yes. But** *that* **was at the time when your** *wife* **was in charge of
the canteen!**

45 /wər + ət + ə, ðə/

A **How terrible! Just imagine,** *we* **were at a concert, enjoying
ourselves, while** *you,* **poor thing, were at the hospital, with a
broken leg!**

B **And a couple of very nice nurses!**

A   **Steven and Mark** are from the **Ministry. Robert and Sam** are
from the **Local Government Offices. And the others** are from a
variety of interested organisations. We're here to discuss
co-ordination. **Who are you?**

B   **Simon and I** are from the **Ministry. The other members of our
committee are coming soon. We're here to discuss** *co-operation*.
And this is *our* **room.**

47   /wəz + frəm + ə, ðə/

A   *This* **was** from the **garden!** *That* **was** from the **garden! And** *this*
was from the **garden! Our own garden! Aren't they superb?**

B   **And look at this! The best of all! This** was from the **garden, too,
was it?**

A   *That* **was** from a **shop.**

B   **No, no, no. I meant** *that*. *That's* **the one I meant – not** *that*.

A   **Good.**

48 /wə + frəm + ə, ən, ðə/

A Old, old letters! How long ago! How romantic! These were from a **General**! These were from an **anonymous admirer**! And **these** were from the **Duke himself**!

B **And these** were from the **Tax Department, I see. Did you ever pay them?**

49 /əv + əs, ðəm + ə(r), wə(r), kən, məst/

A **Only three** of us are **on the short-list, and** *he's* **the favourite.**

B **Surely** *none* **of them can know about his private life? Or they wouldn't** *consider* **promoting him! One of us must do our duty!**

A **If all** of us were **perfect, Martin, I'd agree with you. But I** *must** con*fess* . . .

B **Yes, James? Needless to say, you can trust** *me*! **Absolutely!**

A **I'm glad to hear it. But perhaps more important, in this case:** *You* **can trust** *me* **– I'm sorry to say.**

50 /ðə(r) + ə, wə, wəz + ə, ən, səm/

A **Anything for me?**

B There were some **telephone calls. I said you'd ring back.** There are some **letters. Oh, yes** – and there was an **inquiry. Someone asking about something called Weak Forms. Have we got any?**